SRA Open Court Reading

Reading and Writing Workbook

Workbook 2

Program Authors

Marilyn Jager Adams
Carl Bereiter
Anne McKeough
Robbie Case
Marsha Roit
Jan Hirshberg
Michael Pressley
Iva Carruthers
Gerald H. Treadway, Jr.

SRA

A Division of The McGraw-Hill Companies

Columbus, Ohio

SRA/McGraw-Hill

A Division of The McGraw·Hill Companies

Copyright © 2000 by SRA/McGraw-Hill.

Send all inquiries to:
SRA/McGraw-Hill
8787 Orion Place
Columbus, Ohio 43240-4027

Printed in the United States of America.

ISBN 0-02-661365-4

4 5 6 7 8 9 DBH 04 03 02 01 00

Table *of* Contents

Unit 3

Unit 4

Unit 5

Spelling

bunny

bunnies

1. daisy

2. jelly

3. city

4. party

5. story

6. kitty

7. country

8. buggy

9. grocery

Changing y *to* i *Before Adding Endings* • **Reading and Writing Workbook**

Directions: Change the y to an i and add -es to make each word mean more than one. Write the new word on the line.

Directions: Read each sentence. Look at the underlined word. On the line, write the underlined word so that it means more than one.

1. Jerry found one <u>penny</u>.

   _____

   Susan found five _____.

2. Mom put a <u>pansy</u> in the vase.

   _____

   I put six more _____ in the vase.

3. Mike's <u>daddy</u> helps coach the team.

   _____

   Lots of other _____ help too.

4. Betsy saw one yellow <u>butterfly</u>.

   _____

   Patricia saw three yellow _____.

5. Sally went to a birthday <u>party</u> last week.

   _____

   This week she will go to two birthday _____.

6. Jason ate only one <u>strawberry</u>.

   _____

   Seth ate the rest of the _____.

Name _____

Reading and Writing

1. The boy dug in the mud.

4. She sent me a clock.

2. Ben saw a big ram.

5. My dog Sam likes ham.

3. He took a pen from the box.

6. She wore a wig for fun.

_____
‗‗‗‗‗‗‗‗‗‗‗
_____
‗‗‗‗‗‗‗‗‗‗‗
_____

_____
‗‗‗‗‗‗‗‗‗‗‗
_____
‗‗‗‗‗‗‗‗‗‗‗
_____

_____
‗‗‗‗‗‗‗‗‗‗‗
_____
‗‗‗‗‗‗‗‗‗‗‗
_____

_____
‗‗‗‗‗‗‗‗‗‗‗
_____
‗‗‗‗‗‗‗‗‗‗‗
_____

_____
‗‗‗‗‗‗‗‗‗‗‗
_____
‗‗‗‗‗‗‗‗‗‗‗
_____

Name _____

Unit 1 • Lesson 2

1. The bear was huge.

4. Will Pat go to the store?

2. A plane was high in the sky.

5. Pete has an ice cube.

3. Did Dad read the mail?

6. The sheep are cute.

_____
- - - - - - - - - - - - - - - -
_____
_____

_____
- - - - - - - - - - - - - - - -
_____
_____

_____
- - - - - - - - - - - - - - - -
_____
_____
_____

_____
- - - - - - - - - - - - - - - -
_____
_____

_____
- - - - - - - - - - - - - - - -
_____
_____
_____

Directions: Read the sentences. Draw a line under the words that rhyme.

1. Bob will need to feed seed to the hen.

2. It was fun to run in the warm sun.

3. He was glad he had his dad with him.

4. Joe must latch the catch of the ship's hatch.

5. Sissy will hum while her chum beats the drum.

6. Watch the puppy drag the rag out of the bag.

7. Can you jump over a tree stump?

8. Have you ever taken a trip on a ship?

9. Mom got rid of the old pan lid.

10. Ted tried to grab the tiny crab.

Vocabulary

1. Pam likes to put _____ on her toast.

   ram   jam   tam

2. Please _____ that rabbit in the carrot patch.

   match   batch   catch

3. Dad _____ to work late.

   mad   bad   had

4. This pot is not _____.

   hot   cot   lot

5. The doctor will _____ your neck.

   wreck   check   speck

6. Strong winds _____ snow everywhere.

   blow   mow   crow

7. The bell rang with a loud _____.

   sang   clang   gang

Directions: Read each sentence. Look at the underlined word. On the line, write the rhyming word that makes sense.

Name _____

bookstore	dentist	rabbit
girl	hospital	park
flower	glass	Jennifer
school	father	bed

Person   Place   Thing

_____   _____   _____

_____   _____   _____

_____   _____   _____

_____   _____   _____

_____   _____   _____

_____   _____   _____

_____   _____   _____

Name _____

Megan	elevator	cab
suitcases	city	Chuck
airport	time	apartment

Directions: Read each sentence. Pick a noun from the box that correctly completes the sentence. Write the word on the line.

1. _____ and _____ will visit Grandma.

2. She lives in the _____.

3. Grandma meets them at the _____.

4. They ride in a _____.

5. Soon they are at Grandma's _____.

6. An _____ takes them up.

7. They unpack their _____.

8. It will be a fun _____.

Reading and Writing Workbook • *Nouns*

9

Directions: Add -ed, -ing, -er, or -y to each of the words. Write the new words on the line. Remember to double the last consonant.

-ed

jog _____

sip _____

-er

zip _____

dim _____

-y

mud _____

nip _____

-ing

jog _____

sip _____

-er

hit _____

sad _____

-y

sun _____

chop _____

Spelling

1. Mike is a _____.

   joger   jogger

2. He likes to be outside on _____ days.

   sunny   suny

3. Today many people are _____ in the park.

   running   runing

4. Mike saw his friend Sarah _____ on a bench.

   siting   sitting

5. He _____ and sat down beside her.

   stoped   stopped

6. They ate a _____ snack.

   nutty   nuty

Grammar

hop	gulp	sprint	sip
sob	gaze	shout	leap
weep	jog	whisper	peek

1. drink _____ _____

2. jump _____ _____

3. cry _____ _____

4. run _____ _____

5. look _____ _____

6. say _____ _____

Grammar

Directions: Look at each picture. Read the sentence. Choose the verb that best tells what is happening in the picture. Circle the word and write it on the line.

_____

Seth _____ at the squirrel.

looks peeks frowns

_____

The eagle _____ over the lake.

glides goes moves

_____

Raindrops _____ in the puddle.

pour gush splash

_____

They _____ the canoe.

pushed paddled moved

_____

Dad _____ the bushes every fall.

cuts snips trims

_____

Betty _____ quietly up the stairs.

tiptoes skips stomps

Reading and Writing Workbook • *Vivid Verbs*

Comprehension

1. Pam's new coat is all dirty.
   a. It always looks dirty.
   b. She dropped it in a mud puddle.

2. Tree branches were all over the ground.
   a. A strong wind blew that day.
   b. Birds were building their nests.

3. Mark's white socks are now pink.
   a. Someone played a trick on him.
   b. They were washed with something red.

4. Tammy's bike has a flat tire.
   a. She had run over a nail.
   b. She rode it too much.

5. The puppy was all wet.
   a. It had spilled its water dish.
   b. It had been out in the rain.

6. Brad smelled something sweet.
   a. Mom had baked cupcakes.
   b. Mom had cleaned the floor.

Comprehension

Directions: Read each sentence. Draw a line to the sentence that tells why it happened.

1. Margo runs to the field.

The people moved away.

2. Kevin called his grandmother.

It was too big.

3. Bob's hat covered his eyes.

It is raining.

4. Sam could not open the lock.

He wanted to wish her a happy birthday.

5. Paula could not find her book.

She is late for soccer practice.

6. That house is empty.

She left it at school.

7. Carol grabbed an umbrella.

Her friend had come to visit her.

8. Sue ran to the door.

Her shoes were too small.

9. Alice's feet hurt.

He had the wrong key.

| of | mother | brother | other | one |

1. My _____ and sister are younger than I am.

2. We had _____ hour to write a paper.

3. I had a scoop _____ ice cream.

4. Both my _____ and father work.

5. It is either one or the _____.

Sounds and Spellings

Directions: Circle the correct word to complete each sentence. Write it on the line.

1. You only live _____.

twice
once

2. I _____ my new puppy.

love
dove

3. The store had _____ left.

noon
none

4. Can you _____ over after school?

call
come

5. Would you like _____ more?

some
same

Spelling

Directions: Look at the pictures. On the line, write the blend that will correctly complete each word.

| br | cr | gr | pr | tr | bl | cl | sl | sk | sn | st | fl |

___apes ___ouse ___ag ___ab

___ate ___oom ___amp ___ail

___own ___unk ___ed ___esent

Consonant Clusters • **Reading and Writing Workbook**

Spelling

1. Would you like a _____ of milk?

   grass   glass

2. Adam needs to put a _____ on the letter.

   stamp   clamp

3. A big _____ bear ran into the woods.

   brown   crown

4. This is the sweetest _____ I have ever tasted.

   drum   plum

5. Let's sit under that _____ and eat lunch.

   tree   free

6. Last night Cathy had a funny _____.

   cream   dream

7. Please do not _____ the door.

   clam   slam

Name _____

Spelling

1. blue   pack

_____

2. road   wood

_____

3. snow   berry

_____

4. fire   room

_____

5. every   ball

_____

6. wish   case

_____

7. store   one

_____

8. back   side

_____

9. suit   bone

_____

Compound Words • **Reading and Writing Workbook**

Name _____

1. Marge likes to play base _____ .   line ball

2. Dad put logs in the fire _____ .   fly place

3. Calvin's bedroom is up _____ .   stairs town

4. Mom drives to work on the high _____ .   way wheel

5. Sea _____ floated onto the sand.   weed food

6. Owen ate one black _____ .   board berry

7. Tanna put books in the book _____ .   end case

8. Put on your boots and rain _____ .   coat drop

9. Everyone walked on the side _____ .   walk board

10. A baby plays in a play _____ .   ground pen

Directions: Read the sentence. Choose the word that will correctly complete the compound word and write it on the line.

Vocabulary

Directions: Read the words. Look at the pictures. Write the correct word on the line below each picture. The first one is done for you.

low
lower
lowest

<u>lowest</u>   <u>low</u>   <u>lower</u>

dark
darker
darkest

_____

- - - - - - - - - - -

_____

slow
slower
slowest

_____

- - - - - - - - - - -

_____

rich
richer
richest

_____

- - - - - - - - - - -

_____

Comparatives (er, est) • **Reading and Writing Workbook**

Vocabulary

Directions: Read each group of sentences. Write the word on the line to correctly complete each sentence.

tall   1. George has the _____ snow fort of all.

taller 2. Mike built a _____ snow fort.

tallest 3. Sarah's snow fort is _____ than Mike's.

warm   1. Bill has a _____ hat than Sue.

warmer 2. Al has the _____ hat of all.

warmest 3. Sue has a _____ hat.

loud   1. A cat's meow can be _____.

louder 2. A lion's roar is the _____ of all.

loudest 3. A dog's bark is _____.

wide   1. Mr. Bosker's truck is the _____.

wider 2. Our car is _____.

widest 3. Sue's van is _____ than our car.

Spelling

1. t _____

2. ch _____

3. w _____

4. st _____

1. w _____

2. sm _____

3. h _____

4. c _____

/aw/ = -alk, -all • **Reading and Writing Workbook**

Name _____

1. Jerry and Pam play catch with a _____.

   bawl   ball

2. May we use _____ to color the picture?

   chalk   calk

3. Patty hung a poster on her bedroom _____.

   wall   walk

4. The _____ of corn is five feet tall.

   stall   stalk

5. Our classroom is down this _____.

   hall   hawk

6. I need to _____ to my mother.

   talk   tall

7. Matt and Jeff like to _____ to the park.

   wall   walk

8. Joe wants a _____ slice of cake.

   small   shawl

Directions: Color the pictures.

gray   orange

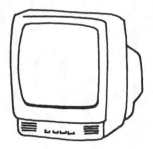  

black   yellow   white

red   green   pink

Color Words • **Reading and Writing Workbook**

Vocabulary

Directions: Read the sentence. Choose the correct color word and write it on the line.

red	blue	yellow	orange	green
	white	black	pink	

1. Vince found a huge _____ pumpkin.

2. My baby sister likes her _____ dress.

3. A seagull flew above the _____ sea.

4. Stars twinkled in the _____ sky.

5. Greg chopped a big _____ tomato for a salad.

6. The little tree had big _____ leaves.

7. The field was covered with _____ daffodils.

8. A blizzard swirled _____ snowflakes everywhere.

Name _____

Vocabulary

write   right   nose   knows   plane   plain

rein   rain   so   sew   wood   would

hole   whole   pale   pail   son   sun

Homophones • **Reading and Writing Workbook**

Vocabulary

1. Tim's team _____ the game.

   one   won

2. We _____ pizza for dinner.

   ate   eight

3. Neville _____ a treehouse.

   made   maid

4. Gloria bought shoes on _____.

   sail   sale

5. Greg must _____ for the bus.

   weight   wait

6. The wind _____ his hat away.

   blew   blue

7. Do you _____ where Bobby went?

   know   no

Directions: Look at each picture. On the lines write oo or u to correctly complete each word.

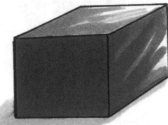

ball__n   c__be   gl__e

m__sic   m__n   st__l

b__t   r__ler   rac__n

Spelling

1. Mark swims in the _____.

   pule   pool

2. The _____ would not pull the cart.

   mule   moole

3. Beth tossed the basketball into the _____.

   hupe   hoop

4. We go to the lunchroom at _____.

   noon   nune

5. Can you _____ this box for toys?

   ooze   use

6. That tiny kitten is so _____!

   coote   cute

7. We need to leave very _____.

   soon   sune

Reading and Writing Workbook • *Compare /Long oo/, /Long u/*

Comprehension

Directions: Read the sentences. Circle the word *Reality* if the sentence tells something that could really happen. Circle the word *Fantasy* if the sentence tells something that is make-believe.

1. Marsha scored the winning point.   Reality   Fantasy

2. The elephant helped the lion pick apples.   Reality   Fantasy

3. Pete Pig and Susie Sow went on a picnic.   Reality   Fantasy

4. David won a prize for reading fifty books.   Reality   Fantasy

5. Rosie swam ten laps in the swimming pool.   Reality   Fantasy

6. A brown chipmunk sat on a stump and ate nuts.   Reality   Fantasy

Name _____

Comprehension

Directions: Read each sentence. If the sentence is fantasy, draw a line under the word or words that tell you it is make-believe. If the sentence tells about something real, write an *R* in the box at the end of the sentence.

1. The tiny baby drove the bus. ☐

2. Sheila took the children to the park. ☐

3. The elf could not find his green hat. ☐

4. Tigers meet at the restaurant for pizza. ☐

5. The hippo rolled in the mud to cool off. ☐

6. Two kittens climbed into the basket. ☐

7. Henry the Hamster put the suitcase in the car. ☐

8. Emma and Ellie fed the fish. ☐

Directions: Read each sentence. Draw a line under the words that begin with a capital letter. Then under the word, write the number that tells why the word begins with a capital letter. 1. It is the first word of a sentence. 2. It is a special name of a person, place, or thing. The first one is done for you.

1. the first word of a sentence
2. the special name of a person, place, or thing

1. My friend Emma went to Chicago.
   <u>1</u>   <u>2</u>   <u>2</u>

2. Please ask Bob to get the newspaper.

3. That elephant came from Africa.

4. Bill's new puppy, Pretzel, is very playful.

5. When are we going to the Children's Museum?

6. Why did Jerry go to Detroit?

Grammar

1. carl and jane rode the train to vermont.

2. three tigers paced inside the cage.

3. grandmother is visiting aunt martha.

4. dick invited adam to his party.

5. ronda saw the play at the newton theater.

6. my cat fuzzy likes to sleep under bushes.

7. did mary ask george to be on the team?

Spelling

Directions: In the first group of words, write -au to complete the word. Then write the word on the line. In the second group of words, write -augh to complete the word. Then write the word on the line.

1. ____ to

2. c ____ se

3. p ____ se

4. bec ____ se

5. t ____ t

6. c ____ t

7. d ____ ter

8. n ____ ty

/aw/ -augh, -au • **Reading and Writing Workbook**

Spelling

Directions: Read each sentence. Circle the word that is spelled correctly. Then write the word on the line.

_____

1. Mom _____ us how to make muffins.

tot   taught

2. Ted missed the show _____ he was sick.

because   becaughse

3. Dad drove his new _____ to work.

auto   otto

4. It is Martha's _____ that we are late.

falt   fault

5. Pat _____ the puppy as it ran past him.

cot   caught

6. We need to _____ these boxes to the attic.

haul   hall

Comprehension

1. They must leave for school now.

2. We can play after we do the dishes.

3. Beth sang as Chuck played the guitar.

4. The calf stayed in the barn during the storm.

5. Kevin fed our cat while we went on a trip.

6. Grandpa will arrive very soon.

7. Sam washed the car before he left.

8. Tina has grown an inch since June.

Directions: Read the sentences. Write the numbers 1, 2, 3, and 4 to tell the order the events happened.

____ Soon he is at the pond.

____ Turtle wakes up as the sun rises.

____ Then he slips into the water.

____ Slowly he walks along the path until he reaches the fence.

____ Everyone cheered as Bruce made the touchdown.

____ He ran down the field until he reached the goal post.

____ He grabbed the ball while it was flying past him.

____ Bruce held up his arms as Pete threw the football.

1. A <u>big</u> <u>yellow</u> (dog) ran into me.

2. The sleepy kitten curled up on the chair.

3. The saw makes a loud buzzing sound.

4. We heard the gentle chimes of the clock.

5. Mom drove slowly down the dusty bumpy road.

6. Andy likes chocolate syrup in milk.

7. Denise put on fuzzy white slippers.

Grammar

Directions: Look at the pictures. Read the sentences. Write the two adjectives that will correctly complete the sentences.

chattering	cold	furry	huge
fluffy	blazing	icy	hot
gray	black	loud	blue

_____ _____

A _____ _____ squirrel ran up the tree.

_____ _____

Meg stood by the _____ _____ fire.

_____ _____

The _____ _____ monkey wanted a banana.

_____ _____

Mike's truck has _____ _____ tires.

_____ _____

Jennifer has _____ _____ earmuffs.

_____ _____

The _____ _____ lemonade tasted good.

1. Sam was next in line.

2. Soon it will begin to snow.

3. Barbara went home after practice.

4. Mike eats dinner later than Steve.

5. Fred swept the floor before he mopped it.

6. Now we should pick up the toys.

7. Lizards sometimes sleep during the day.

8. Cut out the cookie and then put it on the pan.

Name _____

Now   Then   During

_____ we must make a picnic lunch.

_____ Mom will take us to the park.

_____ the baseball game, we can eat lunch.

Before   After   Soon   Next

_____ she finds what she needs to make cookies.

_____ she mixes the dough, she fills the pan.

_____ Amy bakes, she washes her hands.

_____ the cookies are ready to eat.

Reading and Writing Workbook • *Time and Order Words*   **43**

Grammar

foot   feet

mouse   mice

man   men

woman   women

ox   oxen

tooth   teeth

child   children

goose   geese

foot   feet

Irregular Plurals • **Reading and Writing Workbook**

Grammar

Directions: Read each sentence. Choose the correct word and write it on the line.

1. There are two _____ in the store.

   woman   women

2. Ryan chipped a _____ when he fell down.

   tooth   teeth

3. All the _____ cheered for their team.

   child   children

4. Mr. Garson needs four _____ to pull the wagon.

   ox   oxen

5. Sid's dad is a very tall _____.

   man   men

6. Six tiny gray _____ scampered across the floor.

   mouse   mice

7. We had sore _____ after hiking all day.

   foot   feet

Reading and Writing

Directions: Read the paragraph. Write the underlined /j/ and /g/ words in the correct column on this page or the next page.

Gerry the Gardener

Gerry likes to work in the garden behind her cottage. She grows many things like green beans and cabbage. She has the biggest carrots in town. Gerry likes to give her pals Ginger, Gail, and Ginny the things she grows in her garden.

_____

_____

_____

_____

_____

_____

_____

_____

/j/ and /g/ Sounds • **Reading and Writing Workbook**

Reading and Writing

Directions: Read the paragraph. Write the underlined /j/ and /g/ words from p. 46 in the correct column.

_____
- -
_____
- -
_____
- -
_____
- -
_____
- -
_____
- -
_____

Name _____

Spelling

re

build _____   name _____

_____

fill _____   write _____

un

tie _____   kind _____

_____

happy _____   safe _____

pre

view _____   school _____

_____

game _____   pay _____

Prefixes (re-, un-, pre-) • **Reading and Writing Workbook**

Name _____

Directions: Write the prefix *re-*, *un-*, or *pre-* on the line to correctly complete the sentence.

1. Mark had to _____ fold the blanket.

      (fold again)

2. The wobbly tire is _____ safe.

      (not safe)

3. We must _____ clean the wall.

      (clean again)

4. Gus went to the _____ game lunch.

      (before the game)

5. Please _____ fill my glass.

      (fill again)

6. Paula felt _____ lucky when she lost the book.

      (not lucky)

7. Julie had to _____ tie her shoes.

      (tie again)

8. Dad _____ paid for the circus tickets.

      (paid before)

Comprehension

How does Sue feel?

    1. well   2. not well

Why does she feel this way?

    1. She ate too much.

    2. The ride made her dizzy.

    3. The ride was too slow.

How does Christy feel?

    1. sad   2. proud

Why does she feel this way?

    1. She grew the biggest pumpkin.

    2. The judge is smiling.

    3. She is at the fair.

How does Todd feel?

    1. happy   2. upset

Why does he feel this way?

    1. The puppy is being good.

    2. The puppy runs to meet him.

    3. The puppy made a mess.

Comprehension

Pam rubbed her hands while looking up and down the street. She pulled her coat around her and put her hands in her pockets. Sitting on the bench, Pam shivered and waited.

Where is Pam?

___ inside   ___ outside

Draw a line under the words that tell you this.

What is it like outside?

___ cold   ___ warm

Draw a circle around the words that tell you this.

Directions: Read the sentences. Add the best ending punctuation.

1. Can we stop to see the seals _____

2. Randy and Dina jump out of the car _____

3. They buy four tickets _____

4. Randy races down the path _____

5. They can hear loud barking _____

6. How many seals are in the cave _____

7. They watch a seal dive off the rock _____

8. Wow, that seal made a big splash _____

Name _____

Directions: Read the story. Write the correct end marks.

Bonnie looks out the window _____ When is it going

to snow _____ There are lots of clouds _____ It is very

cold _____ Why doesn't it snow _____ Look _____

There is one big white snowflake _____ Soon many

snowflakes are falling to the ground _____ Everything

looks so beautiful _____ Bonnie smiles _____

Reading and Writing Workbook • *Sentence Types*   **53**

1. We watched the chipmunk _____ the tree.

    trim   climb

2. The bird sat on the tree _____ .

    limb   limp

3. Would you like a glass of _____ ?

    winter   water

4. A _____ has a soft coat.

    lamb   lamp

5. I took the dog for a _____ .

    work   walk

Phonics

Directions: Write the sentence that best describes each picture.

The boy jumped in the water.

The boy ran from the wasp.

_____

_____

The lamb walked into the water.

The lion chased the lamb.

_____

_____

The puppy played with the comb.

The puppy ate the crumbs.

_____

_____

Name _____

Spelling

1. talked _____ _____

2. finding _____ _____

3. visited _____ _____

4. leaping _____ _____

5. pushed _____ _____

6. rowing _____ _____

7. filled _____ _____

8. cleaned _____ _____

Base Words with Endings • **Reading and Writing Workbook**

Spelling

Directions: Add -ed or -ing to the base word under each sentence. Write the new word on the line.

_____
1. Todd is _____ his dad rake leaves.

help

_____
2. Marsha _____ to help also.

want

_____
3. Dad _____ her a big bag.

hand

_____
4. She is _____ up the piles of leaves.

pick

_____
5. Dad _____ the bags into the truck.

lift

_____
6. He is _____ to take them to the dump.

go

Name _____

Grammar

1. A little bird made a nest in the tree.

2. The nest was made from twigs and string.

3. Soon there were two eggs in the nest.

4. One day the eggs hatched.

5. The mother bird brings food to the little birds.

6. She puts tiny bits of food into their mouths.

7. Soon the babies start to flap their wings.

Nouns • **Reading and Writing Workbook**

Grammar

friend	apples	boy	bench
bus	cars	time	backpack
snack		game	street

1. Sid sits on a _____ to wait for the _____.

2. He watches _____ go up and down

the _____.

3. Another _____ comes to wait with Sid.

4. He is Sid's _____, Jake.

5. They talk about the baseball _____.

6. Jake takes two _____ out of his

_____.

7. They have a good _____ eating a

_____ as they wait.

Directions: Read the sentences. Choose the correct noun. Write the noun on the line to complete the sentence.

Long I

The sun shines on the jungle. It makes patches of shade and light. A tiger sits in the shadows. Her coat is gold like the sun's light. It has stripes of black like the shade. The tiger blends in with her jungle home.

_____

_____

_____

_____

_____

_____

_____

_____

Review • **Reading and Writing Workbook**

Name _____

Phonics

| read | measure | bread | pleasure | spread |

Treasure _____ _____
_____ _____

Head _____ _____
_____ _____

Directions: Write each word with its rhyming word.

Name _____

Grammar

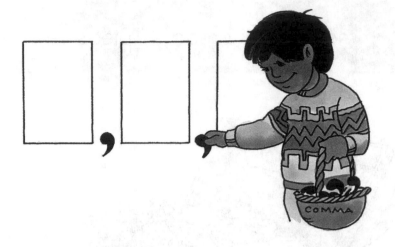

1. They went sledding, skiing, and skating.

2. There was juice, an apple, and a cookie in Mike's lunch.

3. Patty has a dog, cat, and turtle for pets.

4. George needs a pencil, paper, and scissors.

5. Debbie likes to read about baseball, soccer, and football.

6. Megan and Hannah skip, run, and laugh as they walk to school.

Name _____

Directions: Read the sentences. Write the commas where they belong.

1. Sarah sings dances and acts in the school play.

2. Dad is busy sawing chopping and stacking wood.

3. David put the apple pear and orange in the basket.

4. We bought wrapping paper ribbon and bows.

5. Fall leaves turn orange yellow and red.

6. At camp Jed liked hiking swimming and singing songs.

Directions: Circle the beginning consonant blend. Write the consonant blend on the line.

 planet _____   frog _____

 prize _____   brush _____

 fly _____   spoon _____

 gravy _____   crown _____

 skunk _____    block _____

 cloud _____   truck _____

 glass _____   scooter _____

Spelling

1. Sam is my best _____ iend.

   sp   bl   fr   tr

2. The loud bang made the baby _____ y.

   fr   dr   tr   cr

3. We live one _____ ock from the park.

   fl   bl   cl   sm

4. The man unloaded a big _____ ate.

   cr   fr   gr   sk

5. Fred and Jim _____ ay on a soccer team.

   tr   cl   st   pl

6. We saw water _____ ow down the hill.

   sl   gr   cr   fl

7. Chief Todson will _____ eak to us about fire.

   sn   sp   sl   cr

8. Everyone _____ opped to look at the lion.

   fl   pl   st   sl

Spelling

1. Dan got a splinter in his hand.

2. We walked the path to the stream.

3. The quail hid under the shrub.

4. It takes three hours to go to Grandma's.

5. The strong ox pulled the wagon up the hill.

6. Doris forgot to open the screen door.

7. Do you like shredded cheese on pizza?

Spelling

1. Please pick up that _____ ap of paper.

    str   scr

2. Dad will _____ it the log into kindling.

    spl   squ

3. How far can you _____ ow a ball?

    thr   shr

4. A skunk has a white _____ ipe on its tail.

    spr   str

5. Brad's shirt _____ ank and is now too small.

    spr   shr

6. We can _____ inkle coconut on top of the cake.

    spr   shr

7. The _____ ay puppy was cold and hungry.

    spr   str

Name _____

It was lunch time. Huey was hungry. He looked at a

menu and ordered a huge sandwich. Huey had fun as he

waited for his lunch. He watched a lady amuse her cute

baby with a fuzzy toy. He saw a boy argue with his sister.

A few pups jumped up and down outside. At last Huey got

his sandwich. He chewed it happily.

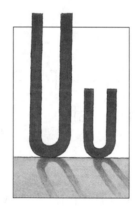

_____   _____

_____   _____

_____   _____

_____   _____

Phonics

1. The puppy (chews choose) on a bone.

2. She only had a (dew few) dollars left.

3. The truck was (hug huge).

4. What a (cute fruit) baby!

5. Please (yous use) the front door.

Name _____

Comprehension

1. Jenny ran and grabbed a paper towel.
   a. She had spilled some juice.
   b. She needed to write a note.

2. Water dripped off the roof at the end of winter.
   a. A water pipe broke.
   b. The sun was melting the snow.

3. Tom blew out all six candles on the cake.
   a. He was afraid of fire.
   b. It was his birthday.

4. Dad bought a new rake.
   a. The old rake was broken.
   b. He liked its blue color.

5. Mom took Shane to the dentist.
   a. He had a chipped tooth.
   b. It was on the way to the store.

6. The dog ran across the yard.
   a. It wanted to look at the flowers.
   b. It was chasing a ball.

Cause and Effect • **Reading and Writing Workbook**

Comprehension

Directions: Read each sentence. Draw a line to the sentence that tells why it happened.

1. Everyone cheered.

2. The sky became very dark.

3. Mom gave Amy some juice.

4. Our car suddenly stopped.

5. Barbara carried the box for Meg.

6. We all sat close to the fireplace.

7. Sid took money out of his piggy bank.

8. Mom handed Georgia some tape.

She was thirsty.

We had run out of gas.

Andy won the race.

It was too heavy for her.

There was going to be a thunderstorm.

She needed to wrap a package.

He was going to buy a gift for Dad.

It was so cold.

Reading and Writing Workbook • *Cause and Effect*

Name _____

Grammar

Directions: Read the sentence. Draw a line under the exact words that are spoken. Circle the word that tells who is speaking.

1. "It is snowing," said Paul.

2. Anne said, "Let's go for a walk."

3. "Put on your hat and mittens," reminded Mom.

4. "A snowflake landed on my nose," giggled Paul.

5. "One landed on my eyelash," laughed Anne.

6. Paul said, "Look, it is starting to stick!"

7. "Maybe we will get lots of snow," said Anne.

Grammar

1. Hurry up, yelled Andy.

2. Here I am, said Amy.

3. Where are your skates? asked Andy.

4. Amy smiled and said, They are in my backpack.

5. Well, let's go, laughed Andy.

6. Hi, Amy and Andy, shouted Sue and Jeff.

7. Let's put on our skates, said Amy.

8. This is a great day for skating! said Sue.

Name _____

Spelling

Directions: Circle the consonant cluster. Write the consonant cluster on the line.

 ant _____

 gold _____

 mask _____

 pond _____

 milk _____

 raft _____

 bolt _____

 heart _____

 lamp _____

 barn _____

Final Consonant Clusters • **Reading and Writing Workbook**

Spelling

Directions: Circle the final consonant cluster that correctly completes the sentence. Write it on the line.

1. This is the be ____ picture Beth has painted.

        nt   st

2. Please a ____ Mark to feed the dog.

      st   sk

3. The truck driver blew the ho ____.

      rn   rm

4. Grandpa lives on a big fa ____.

      rn   rm

5. We we ____ to the zoo yesterday.

      nt   nk

6. Nora wore her new si ____ dress.

      lt   lk

Reading and Writing Workbook • *Final Consonant Clusters*

Directions: In the first group of words, add -s to the word to make it mean more than one. Write the new word on the line. In the second group of words, add -es to the word to make it mean more than one. Write the new word on the line.

s

_____

dog   _____
     _____

clock   _____
     _____

wing   _____

s

_____

book   _____
     _____

car   _____
     _____

nest   _____

es

_____

patch   _____
     _____

inch   _____
     _____

bush   _____

es

_____

guess   _____
     _____

wish   _____
     _____

box   _____

Name _____

Vocabulary

1. Jesse lost her new _____.

    glasss   glasses

2. An alligator has many sharp _____.

    teeth   tooths

3. Little leaves budded on all the _____.

    branchs   branches

4. We filled all the _____ with jam.

    jars   jares

5. All the _____ sat quietly.

    children   childs

6. Dad planted three _____ in the yard.

    treees   trees

Directions: Read each sentence. Circle the correct spelling of the word. Write the word on the line.

Directions: Add -es to the word. Write the new word on the line. Remember to change the y to i.

1. pony _____

2. lily _____

3. fly _____

4. gravy _____

5. city _____

6. hobby _____

7. buddy _____

Spelling

Directions: Add -es to the word under each sentence. Write the new word on the line to correctly complete each sentence.

1. People came from many _____.

   country

2. Do you like _____ on pancakes?

   blackberry

3. They filled the jar with peppermint _____.

   candy

4. Cats have fur to cover their _____.

   body

5. Sue and her friends dressed up like _____.

   fairy

6. Ella won a race after three _____.

   try

Directions: Read the two sentences. Draw a circle around the pronouns. On the line write the words that the pronouns replaced. The first one is done for you.

1. Mary plays with the puppies.

(She) plays with (them.)

2. Bob and I went to visit Grandmother.

We went to visit her.

3. Maggie and Sue waved to Joe and me.

They waved to us.

4. Jeff likes to fly in helicopters.

He likes to fly in them.

5. My brother likes to read to Mom.

He likes to read to her.

1. _____ Mary _____

2. _____ puppies _____

1. _____

2. _____

1. _____

2. _____

1. _____

2. _____

1. _____

2. _____

Pronouns • **Reading and Writing Workbook**

Name _____

Directions: Read the sentence. Circle the words that can be replaced with a pronoun. Write the correct pronoun above the word. The first one is done for you.

I   we   they   us   he   she   it   them   her   him

                    We   them

1. (Betty and I) walk to school with (Sue and Amy.)

2. George wants to drive a bumper car.

3. Missy likes to read funny books.

4. Pat and Chad went on a picnic with Amy and me.

5. The dolphin splashed water on Meg.

6. Loud noises scare Greg.

Reading and Writing

Brad Cooks

It was almost noon. Brad wanted to cook. He took out

a cookbook. He used a big spoon to make the batter

smooth. Then he put his cookies in the oven. Brad used a

broom to sweep up his mess. He shook his apron. When

the cookies were done, he let them cool.

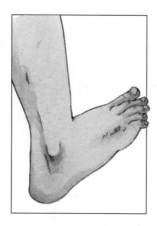

Vowel Sounds and Spellings • **Reading and Writing Workbook**

Directions: Read the story. Then list the long and short oo words in the correct column on this page or the next page. Write each word only once.

Reading and Writing

Directions: Read the story on the previous page. Then list the long and short oo words in the correct column. Write each word only once.

_____
- - - - - - - - - - - - - -
_____
_____

_____
_____
- - - - - - - - - - - - - -
_____

_____
- - - - - - - - - - - - - -
_____

Spelling

Directions: Write -ould on the lines to complete each word. Then write the word on the lines.

1. c _____ _____

2. sh _____ _____

3. w _____ _____

4. c _____ n't _____

5. w _____ n't _____

6. sh _____ n't _____

Pattern -ould • **Reading and Writing Workbook**

Spelling

1. We _____ sweep the porch.

   shood   should

2. The bunny is _____ into the garden.

   runing   running

3. Bobby wishes he _____ go to the park.

   could   cood

4. Dennis _____ the dirty floor.

   mopped   moped

5. Margie _____ like to have a pony.

   wood   would

6. Mom is _____ us some popcorn.

   poping   popping

Reading and Writing Workbook • *Pattern -ould and Double Consonant Endings*

Grammar

Directions: Read each sentence. Draw a circle around the subject of the sentence. Draw a line under the predicate.

1. Morris whistled for his dog.

2. The gray kitten climbed up the tree.

3. Many beavers build dams in that stream.

4. She looks for shells on the beach.

5. Brad found an old picture in the trunk.

6. Samantha and Barb fly kites in the park.

7. Mom gave our dog a bath.

8. A strong wind blew the leaves off the tree.

Sentence Structure • **Reading and Writing Workbook**

Grammar

Directions: Draw a line from each subject to the correct predicate to make a complete sentence.

1. Squirrels   rode a tiny bike.

2. Furry rabbits   makes pizzas.

3. The lizard   gather acorns.

4. A silly clown   hid under a rock.

5. Paul   munch on carrots.

Directions: Write the word that best completes each sentence.

| hair | picture | hear | shore | fire |

1. Did you _____ the bell ring?

2. I will put more logs on the _____ .

3. Dad went to get his _____ cut.

4. Sara drew a _____ of her house.

5. We walked along the sea _____ .

Long Vowels Followed by r • **Reading and Writing Workbook**

Phonics

The store sells teddy bears.

The store sells flowers.

_____

_____

We looked at the pretty pictures.

We could hear the music.

_____

_____

Jane has long, red hair.

Mort poured the mixture.

_____

_____

Directions: Add -ed, -ing, or -er to each of the words. Write the new words on the lines. Remember to drop the e.

ed

wave _____

like _____

taste _____

ing

wave _____

like _____

taste _____

er

frame _____

write _____

race _____

er

time _____

dive _____

tune _____

Adding Endings to Words That End in e • **Reading and Writing Workbook**

Spelling

Directions: Read the sentences. Circle the correct spelling of the word. Write the word on the lines to complete the sentences.

1. Workers _____ our street.

   paveed   paved

2. Mr. Gowns is _____ a rocking chair.

   making   makeing

3. Ms. Wilson is a lion _____.

   tamer   tameer

4. Sam is so cold that he is _____.

   shakeing   shaking

5. Brenda _____ her loose tooth.

   wiggled   wiggleed

6. They are _____ it will snow a lot.

   hoping   hopping

Reading and Writing Workbook • *Adding Endings to Words That End in* e   **91**

Vocabulary

twist	grin	grab	doze
swirl	stumble	hug	grill
snooze	topple	bake	smirk

Directions: Read each word. Look in the box to find more vivid verbs that have almost the same meaning. Write them on the lines.

1. smile _____ _____

2. hold _____ _____

3. sleep _____ _____

4. trip _____ _____

5. spin _____ _____

6. cook _____ _____

Vivid Verbs • **Reading and Writing Workbook**

Vocabulary

The rabbit _____ over the stump.

jumped   sprang   hopped

A big pink balloon _____ over us.

flew   glided   moved

Pam _____ on the door.

knocked   pounded   hammered

Mice _____ across the field.

scurry   hurry   run

The bright star _____ in the sky.

is   appears   sparkles

Reading and Writing Workbook • *Vivid Verbs*

Phonics

| table | candle | supper | cattle | bottle |

1. Dad made meatloaf for _____.

2. We eat dinner at the kitchen _____.

3. The baby drank milk from a _____.

4. She always lights a _____ at night.

5. The _____ graze on the farm.

Phonics

Directions: Write each word next to its rhyming word.

judge	spice	rage	space	twice	budge
cage	race	age	mice	smudge	place

face _____ _____ _____

rice _____ _____ _____

page _____ _____ _____

fudge _____ _____ _____

Vocabulary

Directions: Read each sentence. Look at the underlined word. Draw a circle around the correct meaning of the word.

1. Maggie wants to be in our <u>club</u>.

    a bat   a group

2. Pumpkins get ripe in the <u>fall</u>.

    a time of year   drop

3. This stale cookie is very <u>hard</u>.

    not soft   not easy

4. Mom will be <u>back</u> in an hour.

    rear part   return

5. Jeff stood at the <u>end</u> of the line.

    last   finish

6. Can you <u>name</u> all six food groups?

    what a person is called   tell

7. It will <u>please</u> Mom if we clean up the mess.

    to make happy   a polite word

8. We can make lemonade in this <u>pitcher</u>.

    a person who throws a ball   container

Name _____

Directions: Read each sentence. Look at the underlined words. Read the word meanings. Write the number in the box to tell the correct meaning of the word. The first one is done for you.

1. Mike will <u>play</u> a farmer in the <u>play</u>.

    1. a performance   2. act

2. That <u>story</u> is on the third <u>story</u> of the library.

    1. book   2. floor

3. Please <u>stick</u> this <u>stick</u> in the box with the others.

    1. put   2. a piece of wood

4. Turn on a <u>light</u> so we can see to <u>light</u> the fire.

    1. to set on fire   2. lamp

5. Anne will <u>march</u> in the parade on <u>March</u> 15.

    1. walk   2. a month

Spelling

Directions: Read the word. On the line, write the number of syllables in the word.

1. everlasting _____

2. peppermint _____

3. elevator _____

4. unhappy _____

5. supermarket _____

6. underwater _____

7. helicopter _____

8. afternoon _____

9. library _____

10. buffalo _____

Words with Three or Four Syllables • **Reading and Writing Workbook**

Name _____

strawberries	excellent	November	bicycles
watermelon	motorcycles	ladybug	banana
piano	January	harmonica	elephant
rhinoceros	caterpillar	enjoyable	huckleberries

1. The garage was full of _____.
   (3 syllables)

2. Sam's birthday is in _____.
   (4 syllables)

3. A _____ walked on the green leaf.
   (3 syllables)

4. Pat plays the _____.
   (4 syllables)

5. We made jam with fresh _____.
   (3 syllables)

6. Gloria saw a huge _____ at the zoo.
   (4 syllables)

Spelling

1. play _____

2. farm _____

3. sing _____

4. help _____

5. build _____

6. walk _____

7. spell _____

8. hunt _____

-er *Endings* • **Reading and Writing Workbook**

Name _____

Directions: Add the ending -er to each word to make it mean "something that does the action." Write the new word on the line.

printer

1. dry _____

2. print _____

3. clean _____

4. broil _____

5. stamp _____

6. sweep _____

7. steam _____

8. load _____

Name _____

Spelling

1. turk _____ _____

2. hon _____ _____

3. troll _____ _____

4. k _____ _____

5. hock _____ _____

6. monk _____ _____

ē *Spelled* ey • **Reading and Writing Workbook**

Spelling

Directions: Read the sentences. Circle the word that is spelled correctly. Write the word on the line to complete the sentence.

1. Spilled glue made a _____ mess.

   gooey   gooy

2. Ann slammed the _____ over the net.

   vollyball   volleyball

3. The warm fire made the cabin very _____.

   homey   homy

4. They went on a long _____ across the sea.

   journey   journy

5. Mom put some _____ in the vegetable soup.

   barly   barley

6. Mark saved his _____ for a bike.

   mony   money

Reading and Writing Workbook • ē *Spelled* ey

1. The movie was filled with ac _____.

2. The on _____ had a strong odor.

3. Pay atten _____ in class.

4. Ben won a mill _____ dollars.

5. Don't be afraid to ask a ques _____.

6. We took a long vaca _____.

Phonics

Directions: Write each word next to its rhyming word.

| motion | station | potion |
| billion | vacation | trillion |

1. nation _____ _____

2. lotion _____ _____

3. million _____ _____

Name _____

Grammar

1. wasn't

_____

- - - - - - - - - - - - - - -

_____

2. they're

_____

- - - - - - - - - - - - - - -

_____

3. I'll

_____

- - - - - - - - - - - - - - -

_____

4. hadn't

_____

- - - - - - - - - - - - - - -

_____

5. aren't

_____

- - - - - - - - - - - - - - -

_____

6. she'll

_____

- - - - - - - - - - - - - - -

_____

7. you're

_____

- - - - - - - - - - - - - - -

_____

8. can't

_____

- - - - - - - - - - - - - - -

_____

9. we'll

_____

- - - - - - - - - - - - - - -

_____

10. didn't

_____

- - - - - - - - - - - - - - -

_____

11. they'll

_____

- - - - - - - - - - - - - - -

_____

12. we're

_____

- - - - - - - - - - - - - - -

_____

Directions: Read each word. On the line under each word, write the two words that were put together.

Contractions • **Reading and Writing Workbook**

Name _____

Directions: Circle the two words that can be put together to make a contraction. Write the contraction on the line.

1. Harry must not be late for baseball practice.

_____

- - - - - - - - - - - - - - -

_____

2. Dad said he will fix my bike.

_____

- - - - - - - - - - - - - - -

_____

3. Harriet knows that they are moving soon.

_____

- - - - - - - - - - - - - - -

_____

4. Sam and Eddie do not like scary stories.

_____

- - - - - - - - - - - - - - -

_____

5. Mom said you are going swimming today.

_____

- - - - - - - - - - - - - - -

_____

6. I will put the cookies in the jar.

_____

- - - - - - - - - - - - - - -

_____

Name_____

Vocabulary

Saturday   Tuesday   Friday   Sunday
Thursday   Monday   Wednesday

Directions: Read the names of the days of the week. On the lines, write them in the correct order.

1. _____

2. _____

3. _____

4. _____

5. _____

6. _____

7. _____

Days of the Week • **Reading and Writing Workbook**

Name _____

Directions: Look at the list of days. Read the sentences. Write the name of the day of the week that correctly completes the sentence.

Sunday   Tuesday   Thursday   Saturday

Monday   Wednesday   Friday

1. On _____ we will go to the airport.

2. All of us help clean the house on _____ .

3. Ted will try his new sled on _____ .

4. Everyone will come to dinner on _____ .

5. Mom will go to the grocery store on _____ .

6. It is Grandma's birthday on _____ .

7. On _____ we will go ice skating.

Comprehension

1. Eddie and Sam put up the tent.   Reality   Fantasy

2. Leo Leopard yelled, "I'm going to jog to the park."   Reality   Fantasy

3. Pig carefully drove the tractor to the cornfield.   Reality   Fantasy

4. Rusty walks his dog Dusty every day.   Reality   Fantasy

5. Wanda Wolf read a bedtime story to her cubs.   Reality   Fantasy

6. Rachel helped Mom fold the clean clothes.   Reality   Fantasy

Comprehension

1. Dennis picked some strawberries.

2. Hannah melts when she walks in the hot sun.

3. A big gorilla sat and stared at us.

4. The two monkeys danced and sang.

5. Amy Ant carried the picnic basket to the park.

6. Two puppies tugged on the old blanket.

7. Missy Mouse went shopping for new shoes.

8. Chris shouted, "Wait for me!"

Reading and Writing Workbook • *Reality and Fantasy*

Directions: In the first group, add the prefix *re-* to each word to make it mean "again." Write the new word on the line. In the second group, add the prefix *un-* to each word to make it mean "not" or "opposite of." Write the new word on the line. In the third group, add the suffix *-er* to each word to make it mean "a person who" or "something that does." Write the new word on the line.

re-

pay _____

wash _____

re-

place _____

start _____

un-

fair _____

even _____

un-

taped _____

shut _____

-er

eat _____

mow _____

-er

teach _____

bank _____

Base Words with Affixes re-, un-, -er • **Reading and Writing Workbook**

Directions: Read each sentence and the words in parentheses at the end of each sentence. Write the affix *re-, un-,* or *-er* on the line to correctly complete the sentence.

1. Megan needs to ____ make her bed.   (make again)

2. It is ____ like Barry to be late.   (not like)

3. Dad is a good listen ____.   (one who listens)

4. Sue's coat zipp ____ is stuck.   (thing that zips)

5. Jeff ____ counted his money.   (counted again)

6. Mom will ____ light the lantern.   (light again)

7. Alex put the ____ opened letter on the desk.   (not opened)

8. Ms. Winsler is a good driv ____.   (one who drives)

Name _____

Spelling

Directions: In the first group, add -ure to complete each word. Write the word on the line. In the second group, add -tion to complete each word. Write the word on the line.

-ure

1. pict _____ _____

2. nat _____ _____

3. treas _____ _____

-tion

4. inven _____ _____

5. ac _____ _____

6. frac _____ _____

Spelling Patterns: -ure, -tion • **Reading and Writing Workbook**

Spelling

Directions: Read each sentence. Write *-ure* or *-tion* on the line to correctly complete the word.

1. Eddie asked Mr. Anso a ques _____.

2. The movers unloaded our new furnit _____.

3. Many cows graze in this green past _____.

4. Sam's aunt met him at the train sta _____.

5. Nora likes to read exciting advent _____ stories.

6. They manufact _____ fun toys in that building.

Name _____

1. Ellie listened to the quiet music.

2. Jared and Chris skated down the sidewalk.

3. Snowflakes covered the tree branches.

4. Five raccoons ran into the woods.

5. Grandpa likes reading stories to us.

6. Flashing bolts of lightning zipped across the sky.

Grammar

shine at night   lived long ago
move very slowly   Pat and Sarah
My coat   The diver

Tiny birds | peeked out of the nest.

1. Snails _____ .

2. _____ went skating.

3. _____ found a sunken treasure chest.

4. Huge dinosaurs _____ .

5. Street lights _____ .

6. _____ has two big pockets.

Reading and Writing Workbook • *Sentence Structure*

Spelling

Directions: Add -ous to each word or word part. Write the word on the line.

1. joy _____ _____

2. humor _____ _____

3. nerv _____ _____

4. furi _____ _____

5. gener _____ _____

6. curi _____ _____

7. envi _____ _____

Spelling Pattern: -ous • **Reading and Writing Workbook**

Spelling

1. Mom bakes _____ peanut butter cookies.

   delicious   delicius

2. We saw _____ colorful fish in the tank.

   varius   various

3. Alex is a _____ skateboarder.

   tremendus   tremendous

4. Some plants are _____.

   poisonous   poisonus

5. Peggy is not a _____ person.

   jealus   jealous

6. We all laughed at Bill's _____ costume.

   ridiculus   ridiculous